WEEKLY WR READER
EARLY LEARNING LIBRARY

STORMS
THUNDERSTORMS

by Jim Mezzanotte
Reading consultant: Susan Nations, M.Ed.,
author/literacy coach/consultant in literacy development

Science and curriculum consultant: Debra Voege, M.A.,
science and math curriculum resource teacher

Please visit our web site at: garethstevens.com
For a free color catalog describing Weekly Reader® Early Learning Library's list
of high-quality books, call 1-877-445-5824 (USA) or 1-800-387-3178 (Canada).
Weekly Reader® Early Learning Library's fax: (414) 336-0164.

Library of Congress Cataloging-in-Publication Data

Mezzanotte, Jim.
    Thunderstorms / by Jim Mezzanotte.
      p. cm. — (Storms)
    Includes bibliographical references and index.
    ISBN-13: 978-0-8368-7915-5 (lib. bdg.)
    ISBN-13: 978-0-8368-7922-3 (softcover)
    1. Thunderstorms—Juvenile literature. I. Title.
  QC968.2.M49   2007
  551.55'4—dc22   2006033923

This edition first published in 2007 by
Weekly Reader® Early Learning Library
A Member of the WRC Media Family of Companies
330 West Olive Street, Suite 100
Milwaukee, WI 53212 USA

Copyright © 2007 by Weekly Reader® Early Learning Library

Editorial direction: Mark Sachner
Editor: Barbara Kiely Miller
Art direction, cover and layout design: Tammy West
Photo research: Diane Laska-Swanke

Photo credits: Cover, title, pp. 5, 9, 15 © Weatherpix Stock Images; pp. 6, 7, 18, 21 © AP Images;
p. 10 © Jim Reed/Photo Researchers, Inc.; pp. 11, 12, 13 Scott M. Krall/© Weekly Reader Early Learning
Library; p. 14 © Hank Baker/Weatherpix Stock Images; p. 16 © Onne van der Wal/CORBIS; p. 19
Marvin Nauman/FEMA News Photo

Printed in the United States of America

1 2 3 4 5 6 7 8 9 10 10 09 08 07 06

Table of Contents

CHAPTER 1 **Thunder and Lightning** 4

CHAPTER 2 **Thunderstorms in Action** 8

CHAPTER 3 **Mighty Thunderstorms** 17

CHAPTER 4 **Thunderstorm Safety** 20

Glossary 22

For More Information 23

Index 24

Cover and title page: Lightning streaks across the sky over Richardson, Texas. It hits the ground close to these tall buildings.

CHAPTER 1

Thunder and Lightning

Have you ever seen a thunderstorm? Big storm clouds appear. The sky turns very dark. Suddenly, heavy rain comes down.

During the storm, **lightning** flashes through the sky. Then, you hear loud **thunder**. Strong winds may blow, too. Thunderstorms can be scary!

Lightning is **electricity**. It is a kind of **energy**. It flows through the air, like a river. This energy is the same kind we use to light our homes. Lightning is a lot of energy. One lightning bolt could power millions of lightbulbs!

This thunderstorm starts with rain and lightning.

A thunderstorm brought heavy rain to this city. People look at the flooding that blocks a road.

A thunderstorm can be dangerous. Lightning causes fires. It hurts and kills people. A storm's heavy rain can cause floods.

Sometimes, **hail** falls instead of rain. Hail is pieces of ice. A hailstorm can be like rocks falling from the sky!

Tornadoes may form, too. They are giant tubes of spinning air. Tornadoes stretch down from the clouds to the ground. They can suck things up and spit them out.

Thunderstorms happen around the world. They form in warm, **humid** places. They hit on land and at sea. In the United States, most thunderstorms take place in summer.

The world has millions of thunderstorms each year. Thunderstorms and lightning are happening somewhere in the world every single minute!

Lightning from a storm strikes above this Florida harbor. Florida gets the most thunderstorms in the United States.

CHAPTER 2

Thunderstorms in Action

Thunderstorms start with warm air. The air is full of water. This water is a **gas,** not a liquid. The gas is called water vapor. We cannot see it.

The warm air rises. Higher in the sky, it cools.
The water vapor cools, too. It turns into drops of
water. The drops join together and begin forming
a cloud.

   As the air rises, it pulls up more warm air.
More water drops join together and make larger
drops. The cloud grows bigger very quickly.

A growing storm cloud covers up the summer sky over Texas.

This thundercloud brings heavy rain and strong winds to Manitoba, Canada.

The thundercloud can grow thousands of feet tall. The cloud is full of water, so it looks very dark. The big water drops are heavy. They begin to fall.

The top of the cloud is colder than the bottom. The water vapor at the top turns to ice. Pieces of ice begin falling. They may become hail or turn into rain.

Inside the cloud, warm air keeps rising, bringing up more vapor. At the same time, cold winds blow down from the top of the cloud.

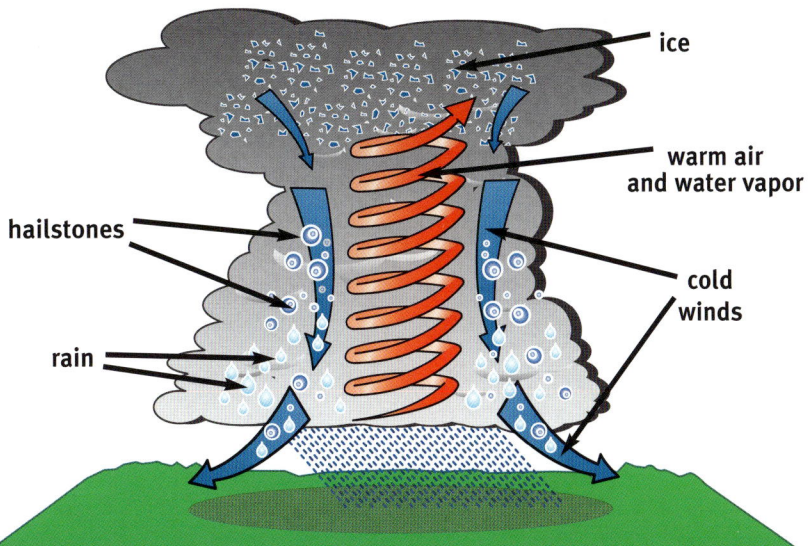

Ice, rain, and hail form inside a cloud. Warm, humid air (*red*) and cold air (*blue*) continue to blow up and down.

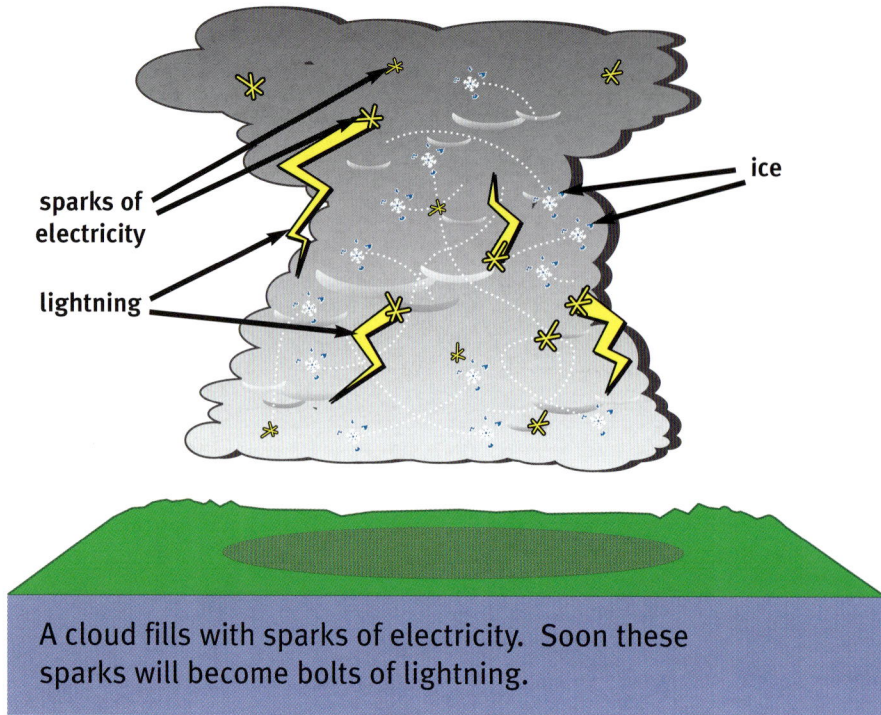

sparks of electricity

ice

lightning

A cloud fills with sparks of electricity. Soon these sparks will become bolts of lightning.

Pieces of ice inside the cloud are blown up and down by these winds. They bump and rub against each other, creating **sparks**. The sparks are electricity that jumps between the ice at the top of the cloud and the ice at the bottom. These sparks become lightning.

When people or things move, they rub against the ground. The air and water vapor around them bump into each other. Just like in a cloud, all these movements create sparks.

The sparks in a storm cloud and those on the ground are drawn toward each other. They meet and form a pathway for the electricity to flow. It flows between the cloud and the ground. We see this electricity as a flash of lightning.

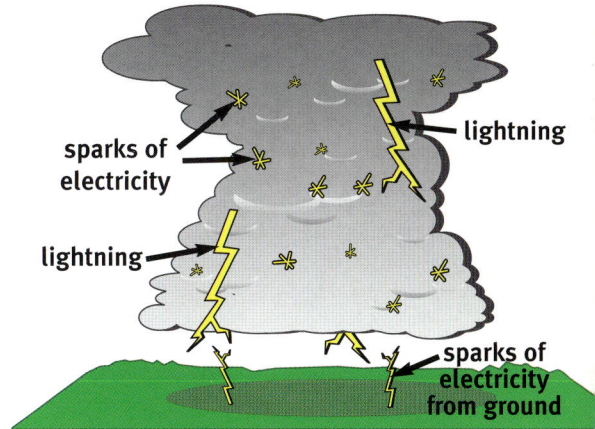

lightning

sparks of electricity

lightning

sparks of electricity from ground

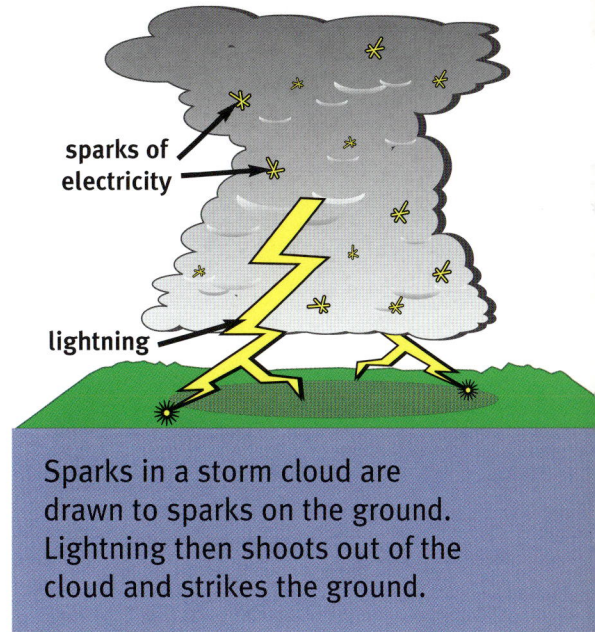

sparks of electricity

lightning

Sparks in a storm cloud are drawn to sparks on the ground. Lightning then shoots out of the cloud and strikes the ground.

A lightning bolt is very hot. It is many times hotter than the surface of the Sun! Lightning's heat makes the air around it explode. Thunder is the sound of this explosion.

Light travels much faster than sound, so first we see lightning. Then, a few seconds later, we hear thunder.

Three lightning strokes hit the ground and heat the air during a summer storm.

Lightning can strike in different ways. It flows between a cloud and the ground. But it can also strike between two clouds or within the same cloud.

Lightning can look like crooked lines. It can also look like a big flash of light in the sky.

These lightning bolts jump from cloud to cloud. They look like fireworks in the night sky.

A dark squall line moves over the ocean. The storm clouds tow a wall of heavy rain toward land.

Sometimes, many storm clouds form in a row. This row is called a **squall line**. As one cloud dies out, another one takes its place.

When the cold winds stop the warm air from rising, a thunderstorm dies out. One thunderstorm can last about an hour. A squall line can last for several hours!

CHAPTER 3

Mighty Thunderstorms

Thunderstorms are powerful. They can cause a lot of damage. Heavy rain may fall in a short time. The rain causes rivers to overflow. Water floods streets and houses.

Hail can damage houses and cars. It can damage farmers' crops.

Lightning often strikes tall things. It strikes trees and buildings. They may catch on fire. Lightning often starts forest fires.

Lightning also strikes people. In the United States, lightning kills almost one hundred people each year. Many people live after they are hit by lightning.

Lightning strikes the Sears Tower in Chicago. The Sears Tower is the tallest building in the United States.

When tornadoes form, they can send cars flying through the air. They can flatten houses. People are often hurt or killed.

A tornado left behind this pile of destroyed homes and smashed cars. A thunderstorm's strong winds often spin into a tornado.

CHAPTER 4

Thunderstorm Safety

Scientists try to keep us safe. They track storm clouds. They warn people when a storm is coming.

During the storm, scientists use a **rain gauge** to measure the rain. The rain falls into a tube. Marks on the tube show how many inches of rain fell. A **weather vane** shows which way the wind is blowing. An **anemometer** (an-uh-MOM-hu-tur) shows how fast the wind is blowing.

A thunderstorm is coming! How do you stay safe? The safest place to be is inside and away from the windows. Lightning can travel through wires and water. Do not talk on the telephone or use a computer. Do not turn on the faucet.

What if you are outside? Stay away from tall trees and open fields. If you are swimming, get out of the water. Do not ride your bike. You can be safe in a car. Learn more about the weather and storms. It will help keep you safe!

A group of people waits under a bridge for a thunderstorm to end. Being outside during a storm can be dangerous.

Glossary

anemometer — a pole with cups that spin in the wind and measure its speed

electricity — a kind of energy. It flows from one thing to another.

energy — power to do things, such as light a home

gas — a form that something can take, such as water. Unlike a solid, a gas cannot hold its own shape. It keeps spreading out. Usually, a gas cannot be seen.

humid — having a lot of water vapor in the air

lightning — a huge amount of electricity that flashes through the air. It may travel between a cloud and the ground, between two different clouds, or within one cloud.

thunder — the sound of air exploding near a lightning bolt

weather vane — a pole with a moveable object on top that spins and points in the direction the wind is blowing

For More Information

Books

Lightning. Seymour Simon (Sagebrush)

Lightning. What on Earth? (series). Brian Williams (Children's Press)

Thunder and Lightning. Watching the Weather (series). Elizabeth Miles (Heinemann)

Thunderstorm. Wild Weather (series). Catherine Chambers (Sagebrush)

Web Site

Web Weather for Kids

eo.ucar.edu/webweather

Visit this site to learn more about thunderstorms and other kinds of storms.

Publisher's note to educators and parents: Our editors have carefully reviewed this Web site to ensure that it is suitable for children. Many Web sites change frequently, however, and we cannot guarantee that a site's future contents will continue to meet our high standards of quality and educational value. Be advised that children should be closely supervised whenever they access the Internet.

Index

air 5, 8, 9, 11, 13, 16
clouds 4, 9, 10, 11, 12,
  13, 15, 16, 20
damage 17, 18, 19
fires 18
floods 6, 17
hail 6, 11, 17
ice 11, 12
lightning 4, 5, 6, 7, 12,
  13, 14, 15, 18, 21
measuring 20

people 6, 13, 18, 19,
  20, 21
rain 4, 6, 11, 17, 20
safety 20, 21
scientists 20
squall lines 16
thunder 4, 14
tornadoes 6, 19
United States 7, 18
water vapor 8, 9, 11, 13
winds 4, 11, 20

About the Author

Jim Mezzanotte has written many books for children.
He lives in Milwaukee, Wisconsin, with his wife and two
sons. He has always been interested in the weather,
especially big storms.